GUIDED**PRACTICE**
ROUTINES**FOR**DRUMS

FOUNDATION LEVEL

Practice With 129 Guided Exercises In This Comprehensive 10-Week Drum Course

BUSTER**BIRCH**

FUNDAMENTAL**CHANGES**

Guided Practice Routines for Drums – Foundation Level

Practice With 129 Guided Exercises in This Comprehensive 10-Week Drum Course

ISBN: 978-1-78933-469-2

Published by **www.fundamental-changes.com**

Edited by Joseph Alexander

www.fundamental-changes.com

Join our free Facebook Community of Cool Musicians

www.facebook.com/groups/fundamentalguitar

Cover Image Copyright: Shutterstock, Evannovostro

Musicians

All audio tracks written and produced by Buster Birch

Contents

About the Author

Buster Birch is an award-winning jazz musician and educator from London, UK. He was a professorial member of the jazz faculty at Trinity Laban Conservatoire of music for seven years, where he taught improvisation, musicianship, jazz repertoire and jazz history classes. He has also lectured at The Royal Academy of Music, The Guildhall School of Music & Drama and Middlesex University.

Buster is a busy freelance jazz drummer who has worked with a great many of the UK's finest jazz musicians. He has an honours degree in music from the University of London and a post-graduate diploma in jazz performance from the Guildhall School of Music and Drama. He also studied at the Drummers Collective in New York City and privately with Jim Chapin and Joe Morello (of The Dave Brubeck Quartet).

He has performed at virtually every concert hall and jazz club in London, as well as major international festivals; he has toured in over thirty countries and recorded nearly forty albums. He has been a member of three world music groups, with whom he recorded and toured extensively, and has played for world-class orchestras including The Royal Philharmonic Orchestra, and deputised on West End shows.

He is director of The Original UK Jazz Summer School, the UK's longest running jazz summer school and winner of the Parliamentary Award for Jazz Education. The summer school is a week-long residential course for singers and instrumentalists of all ages and experience levels.

He is co-founder and leader of BYMT Jazz School which runs weekly jazz improvisation classes for school children at the county music centre. In 2017, BYMT Jazz School won the prestigious Will Michael Diploma Award for Jazz Education – a national award recognising "outstanding commitment to jazz education" and "acknowledging the work of those field practitioners who are actually delivering jazz education and, in many cases, helping to combat the widespread jazz phobia among classroom music teachers and instrumental tutors."

He created his own critically acclaimed show **www.busterplaysbuster.com** which features the Buster Birch Jazz Quartet playing live and in sync to the screening of classic Buster Keaton silent movies, for which he arranged and scored over 4hrs of music. In 2023 Buster plays Buster won the Audience Award at The Chichester International Film Festival – a major UK film festival featuring 110 screenings over 22 days.

Buster is a member of the following bands: ARQ (The Alison Rayner Quintet) – winners of the Parliamentary Award for "Best UK Jazz Ensemble" and the British Jazz Award public vote for "Best Small Group". He is also a member of The Jo Fooks Quartet, Heads South, The London Jazz Trio and The Halstead Jazz Club Big Band.

He has lots of great content, video lessons and free resources for drummers available on his website:

www.busterbirch.co.uk

Buster has written two other bestselling drum books for Fundamental Changes:

The Art of Comping for Jazz Drums

Odd Time Drum Groove Mastery

Introduction

Have you ever listened to a great musician and wondered how they became so good? The answer isn't just talent. Talent only gets you so far. The real difference is *practice*.

As drummers, we need to enjoy making music otherwise, really, what's the point?! But when it comes time to practice, that's when the real work begins. The more disciplined you are with your practice, the more you'll improve, but it's easy to fall into the trap of noodling and messing around during practice time – especially if you don't get much time on your instrument.

The sheer number of things to practice can be overwhelming, and it's easy to waste time deciding what to do. The solution is to have a proper practice routine. Planning your session before you start will give a huge boost to your efficiency. And the only thing better than a planned routine is a *guided practice routine*, which is what this book is all about. You can think of it like having a personal trainer to lead you through each step.

This book is aimed at drummers who can already play some of the fundamental beats, fills and rudiments, but want to refine their essential skills and develop a more solid foundation to build on. You may be self-taught, or not have been playing for very long, and are looking for a complete, practical, structured approach to practicing. This is the book you've been looking for!

How to use this book

As drummers, we always want to work on two main areas of our playing:

- Mastering the drum kit

- Developing musicianship and musical understanding

The routines in this book will help you with the first.

After 42 years of playing drums and over 30 years of teaching, I've found it helpful to divide instrumental skills into three areas:

- Stick control (snare drum technique)

- Coordination (independence of limbs)

- Movement (fluency around the kit)

Taking snare drum exercises and moving them around the kit is a great way to combine stick control, coordination and movement. These routines will do exactly that, alongside other focused drills.

While I was studying at music college, I had the privilege of learning from British jazz drummer Trevor Tomkins, and we spent a lot of time on movement studies – a new concept to me back then. It didn't give instant results, but over time the benefits became clear. My motion around the kit improved dramatically, and that helped my speed, timing and feel. Now it's something I teach to all my students.

There are a few basic principles to follow that will improve your efficiency when moving around the kit, but it's easier to show you this, rather than try to explain it in words. This video on my YouTube channel will guide you through the essential points:

https://geni.us/movingaroundthekit

Don't worry if you struggle with some of these exercises at first – that's expected. You're not supposed to play everything perfectly on the first attempt. (If you can, then you probably need the next book!) A week is a good amount of time for each routine, but you can extend it. After two weeks, move on; you can always come back later.

You don't need to follow these routines in order – just pick one and stick with it every day for at least a week.

The routines in this book cover the essential skills and techniques required for drum grades 1-3. As such, you will find many of the exercises work well as complementary studies for the exam repertoire.

Now, let's get started!

Buster

How to Read the Drum Notation

The musical notation in this book uses the following system to show which parts of the drum kit are played in an exercise or groove.

Notation key:

Drum Notation Guide

| Crash Cymbal | Hi-Hat | Hi-Hat Open | Hi-Hat Closed | Ride Cymbal | Hi Tom | Mid Tom | Snare Drum | Rim Click | Low Tom | Bass Drum | Hi-Hat Foot |

An Important Note on the Lessons and Audio

Each chapter in this book is designed as a complete practice routine.

The accompanying audio can be played as a continuous track, guiding you through the exercises in sequence with spoken instructions between each one. Or, if you prefer to focus on a specific exercise, you can also play the audio tracks individually.

To make this flexible, the narration for each exercise has been *placed at the end of the previous track*. In other words, the introduction to Example 1b is heard at the end of the Example 1a audio track. This allows you to skip directly to an exercise without hearing the spoken introduction, or include it when playing the routine from start to finish.

Use the audio in the way that best suits your practice style. You can run the full routine or isolate a single challenge!

Get the Audio

The audio files for this book are available to download for free from **www.fundamental-changes.com.** The link is in the top right-hand corner. Click on the Drums link then simply select this book title from the drop-down menu and follow the instructions to get the audio.

We recommend that you download the files directly to your computer, not to your tablet, and extract them there before adding them to your media library. On the download page there are instructions, and we also provide technical support via the contact form.

www.fundamental-changes.com

Join our free Facebook Community of Cool Musicians

www.facebook.com/groups/fundamentalguitar

Tag us for a share on Instagram: **FundamentalChanges**

Routine One – 1/8th Notes

Let's start with the first three classic rudiments: singles, doubles and paradiddles. First, listen to the audio introduction for Routine One.

Focus on playing evenly spaced notes with a consistent tone. Aim to strike the same spot on the drum (dead centre) with both sticks and keep the stick heights equal for both hands. Watch the dynamics and use stick height to control the volume for each dynamic marking.

Example 1a

Now add the bass drum on all four beats to introduce some coordination. Make sure every bass drum note is even and that you're following the dynamic markings. Listen to the audio to hear how it should sound.

Example 1b

Next, add the toms to turn this into a movement exercise. The sticking patterns allow for open-handed movement around the kit. Avoid returning your hands to the start position after each stroke. Keep your hands out as you move around the kit and make your movements as efficient as possible. Play the full exercise three times at *mf*, *f* and *p*.

Example 1c

Now add the bass drum on all four beats to combine technique, movement and coordination. Play the exercise three times at *mf, f* and *p*.

Example 1d

This next example introduces a rhythmic idea you'll use later for fills. Start on the snare drum, then add the bass drum on each beat. Follow the changes in dynamics closely.

Example 1e

Now move around the toms while repeating each bar. Follow the dynamic markings as they change.

Example 1f

This coordination exercise focuses on control between your hands and right foot. Aim for an even sound across all strokes with no accents.

Example 1g

Staying with 1/8th notes, let's work on the coordination between your right hand, right foot and left hand. Play the exercise twice, first with the right hand on the hi-hat, then repeated on the ride cymbal.

Example 1h

This next example combines the three key ingredients that will appear in the grooves at the end of this routine. Working in 2/4 helps us isolate and understand the rhythmic elements of 4/4 grooves. First play on the hi-hat, then move to the ride cymbal for the second time.

Example 1i

The next two exercises cover some orchestration options for the first two fills, based on the two rhythmic motifs you played earlier. Pay attention to the sticking – it'll help you to move smoothly around the kit.

Example 1j

Now apply the second rhythmic motif using the same structure.

Example 1k

Let's finish by putting some of these grooves and fills together into a 4/4 loop. For each fill, use the suggested rhythmic motif but experiment with the orchestration by playing the snare and toms in a different order. Repeat the whole exercise and switch to the ride cymbal the second time.

Example 11

Now go back through the grooves again, this time using the other rhythmic motif for your fills.

Example 1m

Well done! You've completed the first routine.

If you found this challenging and want to spend a few more days (or even another week) on it, that is absolutely fine – take your time. But after two weeks, move on. You can always return to this routine later, and when you do, you'll notice that it feels easier because your skills will have improved.

If, after a few days of working on this routine, you feel ready to move on, don't! Stick with one routine and play it every day for at least a week, then review it. This is important because you're programming good habits and that takes repetition.

Remember the adage: don't practice until you get it right. Practice until you can't get it wrong. There's a big difference!

Routine Two – 1/8th Notes, Accents and 1/16th Note Fills

These first few exercises explore accents over single strokes, switching between both hands. Aim for even dynamics. The goal is to make every accented note the same volume, whichever hand it's on, and every unaccented note the same volume, whichever hand it's on. Keep the unaccented notes as low as possible. Use stick height to help with this. If both hands are at the same height, the volume is much more likely to be even.

Example 2a

Now add the bass drum. At first, you might find it challenging to play the left-hand accents against the right foot. Slow down and repeat this as many times as you need. It might even take a few days to get it. That's completely normal.

Example 2b

Repeat the first exercise, this time with movement around the kit. The left-hand accents require some crossing of your hands, which can be tricky at first, especially the switch back to the right hand on the repeat. Aim for dead centre on each tom and keep the unaccented snare notes low.

Example 2c

Now add the bass drum again to challenge your coordination but don't play it too loudly. The toms should sing out clearly above it.

Example 2d

These next exercises introduce two more rhythmic ideas that you'll use for fills later in this routine. Start on the snare drum, then move the figure around the toms. Watch for the changes in dynamic markings.

Example 2e

Now add the bass drum.

Example 2f

Take note of the sticking pattern in the next figure. It keeps the beat on your right hand. Again, make sure you're following the dynamics.

Example 2g

Now add the bass drum to this figure.

Example 2h

This next hand and foot exercise adds doubles and paradiddles. Play the hi-hat the first time, then switch to the ride.

Example 2i

The next exercise introduces the four basic elements you'll use in all the grooves at the end of this routine. Start on the hi-hat and move to the ride cymbal the second time through.

Example 2j

The next two exercises give orchestration options for the upcoming fills, based on rhythmic motifs you've already used.

Example 2k

Pay close attention to the sticking in this next exercise. Playing the two 1/16th notes as R L allows you to land on the crash with your right hand.

Example 21

Now let's combine some of those grooves and fills into a 4/4 loop. For each fill, use the suggested rhythmic motif, but mix up the orchestration by playing the snare and toms in a different order. Repeat the whole exercise and move to the ride cymbal on the second time through.

Example 2m

Repeat the grooves again, this time using the other rhythmic motif for your fills.

Example 2n

You've completed the second routine!

That's all the essential one-beat fills and 1/8th note grooves covered. Next, we'll move on to 1/16th note exercises.

Routine Three – 1/16th Note Singles and Doubles

This routine focuses on 1/16th note singles and doubles, finishing with a set of 1/16th note grooves. Let's begin on the snare drum. Focus on playing evenly spaced notes with a consistent tone. Pay attention to the dynamics and use stick height to control the volume for each marking.

Example 3a

Now add the bass drum to introduce some extra coordination.

Example 3b

Let's add some movement around the kit using the same singles and doubles pattern. Before you start, take a moment to look at the movement sequence on the last line.

Example 3c

Now add the bass drum again to increase the coordination challenge.

Example 3d

The next four exercises introduce 1/8th note accents within the 1/16th note patterns. This means that all accents land on the right hand. Start on the snare drum and play each line twice.

Example 3e

Now add the bass drum to the same exercise.

Example 3f

Now play the same sequence around the toms to include some movement studies.

Example 3g

Next, add the bass drum to this sequence.

Example 3h

Now let's move over to the hi-hat and work on accent placements. When playing accents on the hi-hat, stay relaxed and use technique, not strength, for the louder notes.

Play all unaccented notes on the top of the hi-hat using the tip of the stick. Play all accented notes on the edge of the hi-hat using the side of the stick. Aim to strike with the thicker part of the stick where the taper ends. Keep your hand up and away from your body. Find the sweet spot where you can switch between both strokes with minimal hand movement.

Be careful not to accent the bass drum when you accent the hi-hat. All bass drum notes should be as even as possible.

Example 3i

Now apply the same technique to 1/16th note hi-hat strokes. Play all left-hand notes on the top of the hi-hat with the tip of the stick, and make sure you keep your left hand up.

Example 3j

This next exercise covers the three basic ingredients you'll use in the grooves at the end of this routine. First, play them all on the edge of the hi-hat with the side of the stick. Then, on the repeat, play them all on the top of the hi-hat with the tip of the stick. It's important to be able to use both techniques in a controlled way.

When playing snare drum notes, move your right hand fully across to strike the centre of the snare drum.

Example 3k

Let's end this routine with some grooves built from the ingredients above. Use the suggested rhythmic phrasing for each fill, but improvise how you orchestrate the fill around the kit.

Example 31

Repeat the grooves again, this time using the other rhythmic motif for your fills.

Example 3m

Routine Four – 1/16th Note Paradiddles, Accents and Combinations

This routine focuses on 1/16th note paradiddles, accent placement and combinations of stickings. It finishes with the remaining 1/16th note grooves. Let's begin on the snare drum. Focus on playing evenly spaced notes with a consistent tone. Watch the dynamics and use stick height to control the volume for each marking.

By combining singles and doubles, you can create interesting sticking patterns. The paradiddles flip the lead hand, which adds variation.

Example 4a

Now add the bass drum and stay alert for when the paradiddle flips the sticking.

Example 4b

Let's move this to the toms so you can hear the melodies the sticking patterns create.

Example 4c

Now add the bass drum. Be careful when the paradiddle flips the sticking – your right hand will naturally want to follow your right foot.

Example 4d

The next four exercises combine 1/8th notes and 1/16th notes using singles, doubles and paradiddles. Be careful not to rush the 1/16th notes when switching from 1/8th notes. Keep your focus on the quarter note pulse and aim to lock in with that groove.

Example 4e

Now add the bass drum. Check where the left hand lands in relation to the bass drum notes.

Example 4f

Now move the 1/8th notes to the toms to create melodic phrases.

Example 4g

Now add the bass drum.

Example 4h

Next, you'll add accents to the beginning of each paradiddle. Play the unaccented notes on the snare as quietly as you can and strike the toms dead centre. Use stick height to help maintain consistency in your dynamics.

Example 4i

Now add the bass drum.

Example 4j

This next exercise includes the four basic ingredients you'll use in the grooves at the end of this routine. First, play everything on the edge of the hi-hat with the side of the stick. Then, on the repeat, play everything on the top of the hi-hat with the tip of the stick. Always move your right hand fully over to strike the centre of the snare drum.

Example 4k

To finish, play some grooves using the above ingredients. Play each exercise twice and use the given rhythmic phrasing for each fill. Improvise your orchestration around the kit; there are many variations available.

Example 4l

Example 4m

Routine Five – Triplets

This routine focuses on 1/8th note triplets and introduces paradiddle-diddles and double paradiddles. All grooves and fills are in a 12/8 time signature, which is common in blues and pop ballads.

Because three is an odd number, using single strokes for triplets causes the sticking to switch on each beat. It's important to get comfortable playing the pulse with either hand. As you play, think of your right hand covering beats 1 and 3, and your left hand on 2 and 4. You can also use double strokes to keep the sticking lead on the right hand.

Pay close attention to dynamics in the next few exercises and aim for even strokes with no accents.

Example 5a

Now add the bass drum.

Example 5b

As you move the triplets around the toms, you'll discover the challenge of crossing your hands, especially when moving from the floor tom back to the snare. Start slowly and keep your movements as efficient as possible.

Example 5c

Now add the bass drum.

Example 5d

The next exercise introduces the paradiddle-diddle, but probably not how you've done it before. Thinking of them as triplets makes them much more useful for grooves and fills. When you add the bass drum, it'll help highlight the triplet feel. Notice how the sticking keeps the right hand on the pulse.

Example 5e

Now play what's known as right-hand lead. Moving your right hand onto the toms brings out the melodic phrase created by the sticking. Instead of counting every note, focus on the right-hand melody and let your left hand fill in the gaps. Play all snare drum notes quietly so the melody in your right hand stands out. It repeats every two beats.

Example 5f

Now you're going to play double paradiddles as triplets. This creates a more complex pattern as the pulse shifts from right to left and back. When you add the bass drum, the coordination becomes more challenging. Take your time and practice it slowly. It might take a few days before you can play it comfortably at tempo.

Example 5g

Now play right-hand lead again. This time the sticking forms a longer melodic phrase that fits over four beats. When you add the bass drum, the result has an Afro-Cuban feel. This pattern is very close to a Bembé rhythm – a classic Afro-Cuban rhythm.

Example 5h

Next, work on triplet unisons – a common element in classic rock fills. Be careful not to flam the sticks as you move around the kit. Aim for the centre of each tom.

Example 5i

This next exercise takes you through all the downbeat and upbeat bass drum placements in 6/8 time. These are the basic ingredients you'll use for the 12/8 grooves at the end of this routine. First, play using hi-hats, then repeat on the ride cymbal.

Example 5j

Now practice triplet fills. The metre has changed here and each beat is now 50% longer, so none of the previous fills will fit.

This creates a new rhythmic language, which means new fills to learn. These fills use a mix of 1/8th notes and 1/16th notes and move through every combination systematically. Only a few orchestrations are shown, but many more are possible for each rhythm.

Example 5k

To finish, play some grooves and fills in 12/8 using combinations from the previous two exercises. Each fill gives you a rhythmic phrase, but you can choose which drums to play. These grooves and fills are often used in blues and pop ballads.

First, play using hi-hats, then repeat the exercise on the ride cymbal.

Example 51

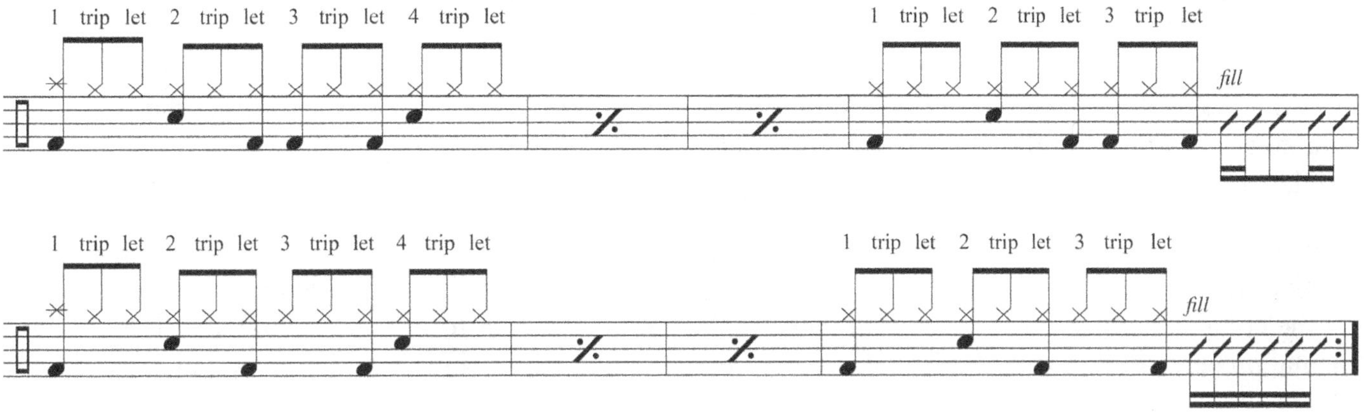
1 trip let 2 trip let 3 trip let 4 trip let
1 trip let 2 trip let 3 trip let
fill
1 trip let 2 trip let 3 trip let 4 trip let
1 trip let 2 trip let 3 trip let
fill

Routine Six – Shuffles

This routine continues with triplets and introduces accent phrasing. The grooves and fills at the end of this routine are based on shuffle patterns, which are common in Rhythm and Blues, Rock, Rock and Roll, and similar styles.

Accents can be used to create melodic phrases on the drums. While playing continuous strokes, you can emphasise either hand to form patterns that span several beats or bars. When playing phrases like this, focus on the complete phrase rather than each individual note. I often refer to this as zooming out. It's the same mental process you use when reading this sentence; your brain reads whole words, not individual letters.

By accenting all of the right-hand or all of the left-hand strokes in triplets, you create a 3-over-2 polyrhythm. Play the unaccented notes as quietly as possible, and use stick height to keep dynamics consistent. Use full strokes for the accented notes and keep the sticks very low for the unaccented notes.

Example 6a

Now add the bass drum. Watch out for the left-hand accents against the right foot in the sixth bar.

Example 6b

52

Now move the exercise around the kit. Be careful at the end when your hands cross over in the sixth bar.

Example 6c

Now add the bass drum.

Example 6d

The next exercises introduce the R L R sticking. This will give you a strong foundation for the shuffle grooves at the end of this routine.

Example 6e

Now move the exercise around the kit.

Example 6f

Now combine the shuffle sticking pattern with the right-hand 3-over-2 polyrhythm to create more complex phrasing.

Example 6g

Now move that around the kit using the orchestration provided.

Example 6h

The next exercise includes shuffle unisons on the snare and toms. These are often heard in classic rock fills. Be careful not to flam the sticks and strike the centre of each tom.

Example 6i

This exercise covers all the downbeat and upbeat bass drum placements within a shuffle. These are the core elements you'll use in the grooves at the end of this routine. First, play using hi-hats, then repeat the whole thing using the ride cymbal.

Example 6j

Shuffle beats are usually faster than the 12/8 triplets used earlier. This means there's not enough space to include 1/16th notes in the fills, so we use 1/8th note triplets instead. It's common to include an upbeat pick-up note in a shuffle fill, so the first two fills start on each beat, then repeat with a pick-up note.

Example 6k

Finally, you're going to end this routine with some shuffle grooves and fills, combining the ideas from the previous two exercises. Each fill includes a rhythmic phrase, but you choose the drums. These grooves and fills are frequently heard in Rhythm and Blues, Rock, Rock 'n' Roll, and related styles. First, play using hi-hats, then repeat the exercise on the ride cymbal.

Example 61

Routine Seven – 1/4 Notes, 3/4 Time, and Hi-Hat Lifts

This routine incorporates a mix of exercises, from 1/8th note accent phrases to 3/4 grooves, what I refer to as "changing gears", plus hi-hat lifts and 1/4 note grooves.

Let's begin with some 1/8th note accent phrases. As you play, zoom out and listen to the full phrase rather than focusing on each individual note. When you move to the toms, concentrate on the melody they create. Play the unaccented snare notes as quietly as possible.

Example 7a

Now add the bass drum.

Example 7b

The next four exercises explore some simple grooves and fills in 3/4 time signature. Most people find 3/4 a bit challenging at first, simply because it is unfamiliar. After all, nearly all of the popular music we hear is written in 4/4 time signature, so 3/4 can feel a bit strange. You just need to familiarise yourself with the common placements.

Instead of using a lot of energy to concentrate on counting the beats, focus your mind on the melody that the bass drum and snare drum placements create. Once you get used to the sound of each melody looping, then it is much easier to play the rhythms.

Start with just the snare drum and bass drum, so you can really hear the melodies.

Example 7c

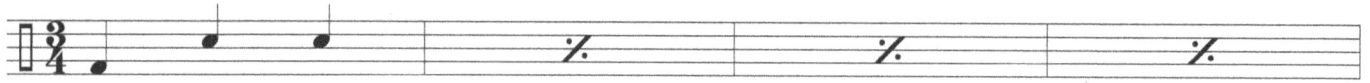

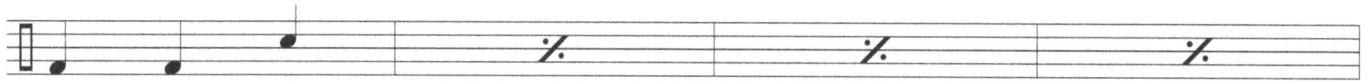

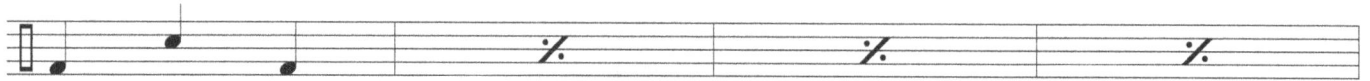

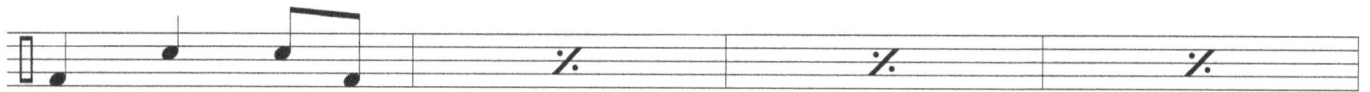

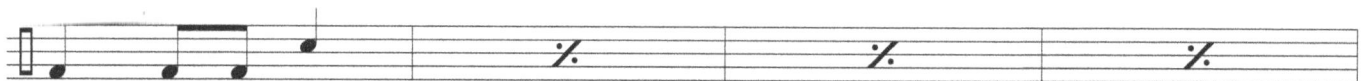

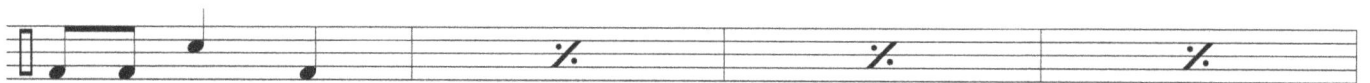

Now add 1/4 notes on the hi-hat with your right hand. This will add some coordination to the exercise.

Example 7d

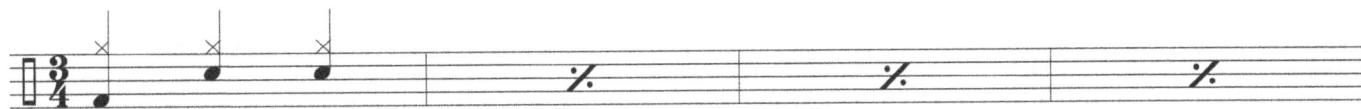

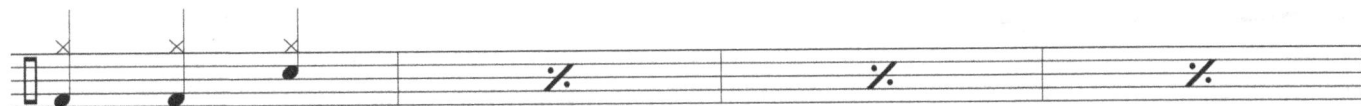

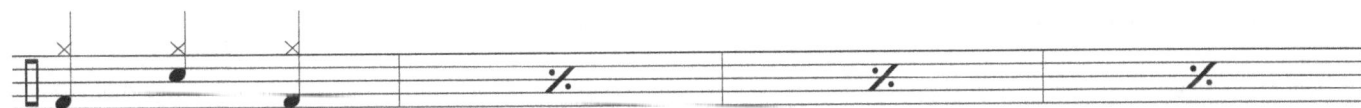

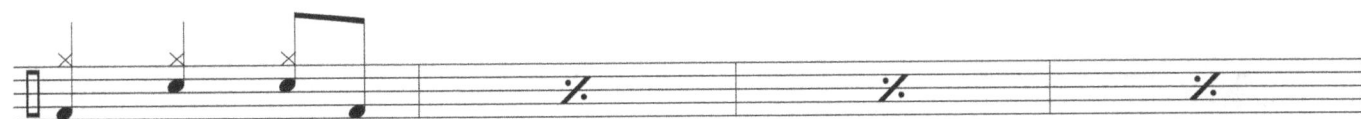

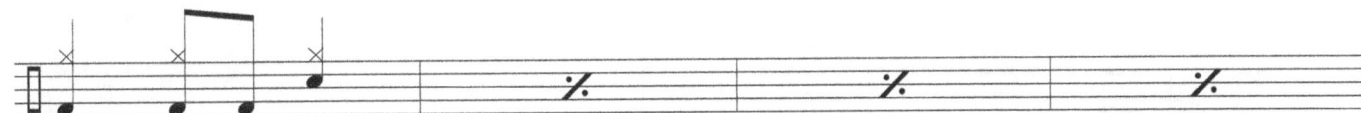

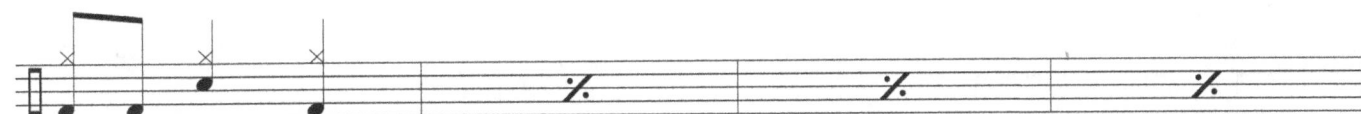

Now play 1/8th notes on the hi-hat, like a regular groove, and add some fills at the end of each line.

Example 7e

Finally, play 1/16th notes on the hi-hat using both sticks and add some fills at the end of each line.

Example 7f

The next two exercises focus on what I call *changing gears*. This refers to shifting the energy of the music. For example, going from a verse to a chorus, or from a chorus to a bridge.

First, practice the right-hand movements. This kind of approach works well in rock or heavier rock songs. Start with regular hi-hat notes, then move to half-open (or trashy) hi-hats, then transition to riding the crash cymbal.

Example 7g

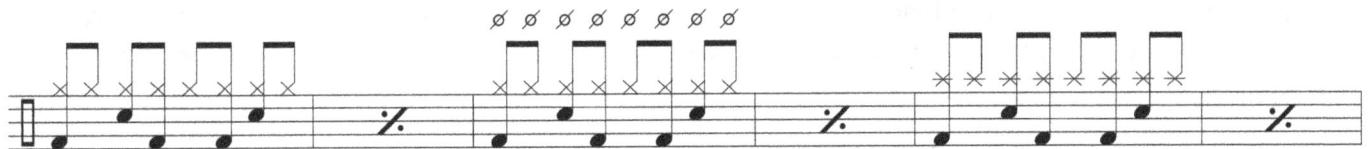

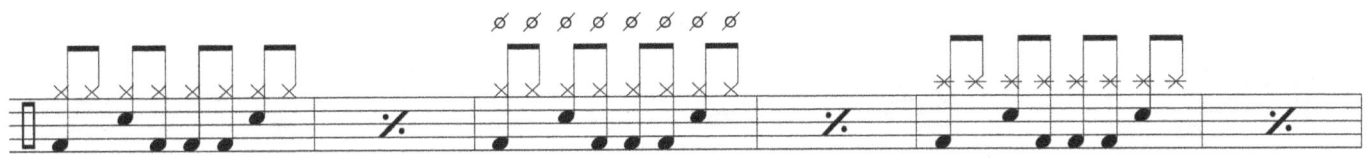

Now combine left- and right-hand moves. Start with rim clicks on the left hand, move to regular snare drum strokes, then shift the right hand to the ride cymbal. These gear changes are especially useful in pop or soul ballads.

Example 7h

The next two exercises introduce the hi-hat lift technique. Always play a lift with the edge of the stick, not the tip, and strike just before the hats are fully open. You want to hear the sizzle between the two cymbals. If you wait too long, you'll only hit the top cymbal, which sounds thin and tinny.

The left foot closing stroke is shown with a plus sign above the note.

Start with just the hi-hat, focusing on the timing between your right hand and left foot.

Example 7i

Example 7j

Now add the bass drum. Timing is critical here. Your left foot should close the hi-hat at exactly the same time your right foot hits the bass drum. Avoid any flam between them.

Example 7k

The next exercise reverses the coordination with your feet. Now your left foot should open the hi-hat at the same time as your right foot plays the bass drum.

Example 7l

This next exercise takes you through all the downbeat and upbeat bass drum placements in a 2/4 time signature. These are the essential components you'll use for the 1/4 note grooves at the end of this routine.

At first, you might feel your right hand wanting to follow your right foot and vice versa. Count "one and two and" for each bar to keep a mental grid for timing. This will help your coordination.

First, play the exercise on the hi-hats, then repeat using the ride cymbal.

Example 7m

Finally, finish this routine with some grooves and fills in 4/4 time, using a combination of the previous two exercises. Each fill includes a rhythmic phrase, but you choose which drums to use. These fast 1/4 note grooves are often heard in Punk, Ska and Rockabilly.

First, play the exercise on the hi-hats, then repeat it using the ride cymbal.

Example 7n

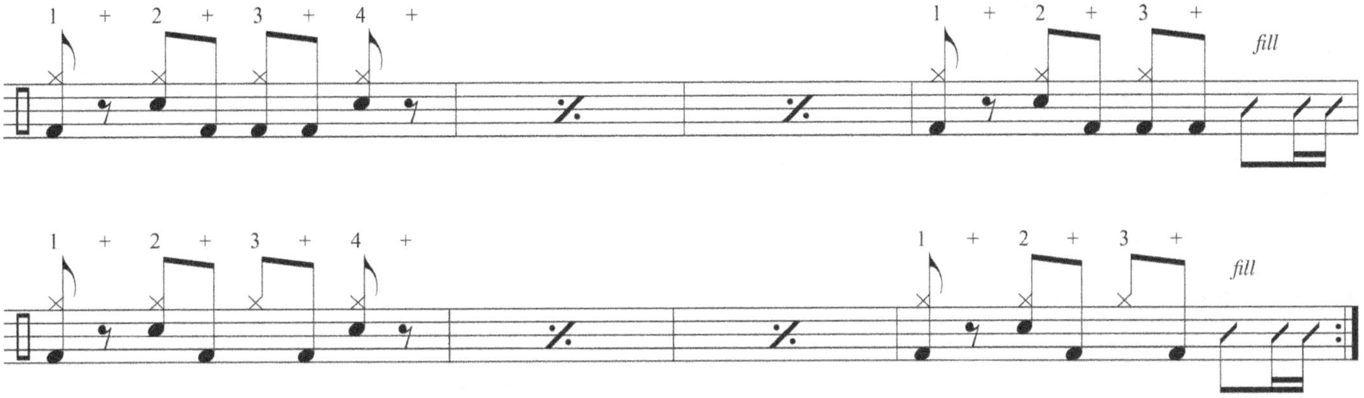
1 + 2 + 3 + 4 +
1 + 2 + 3 +
fill
1 + 2 + 3 + 4 +
1 + 2 + 3 +
fill

Routine Eight – Flams, Crashes and Hi-Hat Lift Grooves

This routine introduces flams, both as technical studies and incorporated into fills, as well as playing crashes on different beats, and using the hi-hat lift in 1/8th note grooves.

First, let's begin with some more 1/8th note accent phrases. Focus on the melody as you move to the toms, and play the unaccented snare drum notes as quietly as possible.

Example 8a

Now add the bass drum.

Example 8b

Next, you'll work on flams. When playing flams, keep your focus on the main note (the big one), not the grace note (the small one). This can be tricky because the grace note takes more skill to execute, so your brain naturally wants to focus on it.

I've provided the stickings for the main notes only, as that's where your attention should be. The grace notes are always played with the opposite hand. Flip the stickings when you repeat each exercise.

Example 8c

Play the opposite sickings on repeat

The next exercise uses double strokes and moves around the drums. This rudiment is traditionally called *flam taps*.

Example 8d

Play the opposite sickings on repeat

Now play the bass drum in the gaps between the notes – a technique sometimes used in rock and pop fills.

Example 8e

Flammed 1/4 note triplets work well for classic rock fills. Start on the snare drum and make sure the notes are evenly spaced. This creates the illusion of stretching the time.

Example 8f

1st x LR 2nd x RL

74

Now use flams with some standard fills. If you have multiple crash cymbals, alternate between them as you play.

Example 8g

The next exercise helps you get comfortable playing crashes before and after beat one. Anticipating the beat is often called "pushing the one". When you crash after beat one, it's usually a good idea to set it up with a downbeat to cue the band. The snare works well for this, but you can also use a tom.

Example 8h

The last four exercises work on four-limb coordination, using the hi-hat lifts introduced in the previous routine.

Don't just think about where the hi-hat opens – it's equally important to pay attention to where it closes (shown by the plus symbol) and what your right foot is doing at that moment.

When you include a hi-hat lift in a groove, you draw attention to the note that follows: the closing point of the hi-hat. This puts emphasis on that part of the groove, whether it's the downbeats or the upbeats. Rock drummers often use hi-hat lifts landing on beat one to highlight the bass drum downbeats. Funk drummers tend to use lifts landing on beats two and four to emphasise the snare backbeats.

The first exercise uses 1/8th note bass drum placements with hi-hats closing on beat one. The plus sign on the first beat of the first bar becomes relevant once the bar repeats.

Example 8i

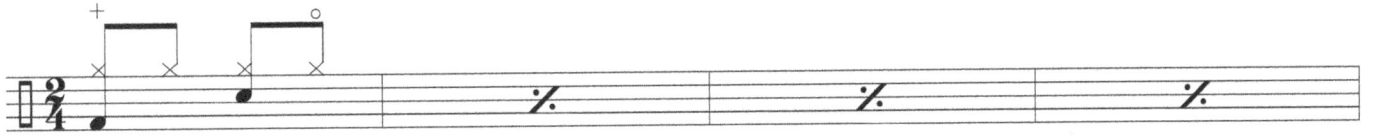

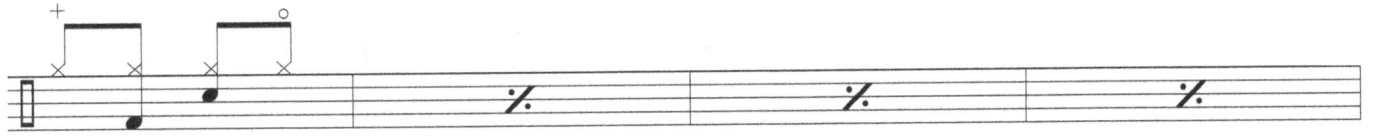

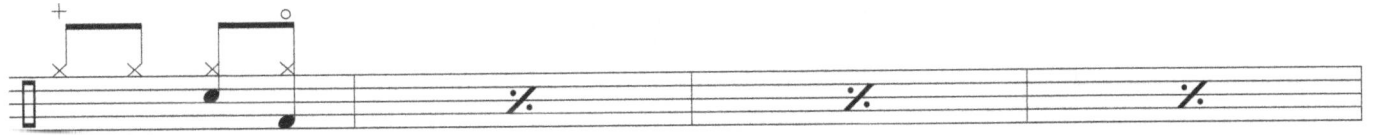

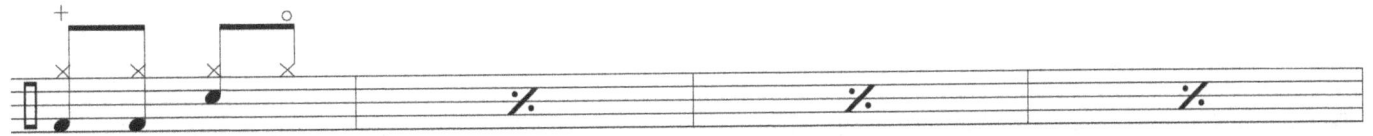

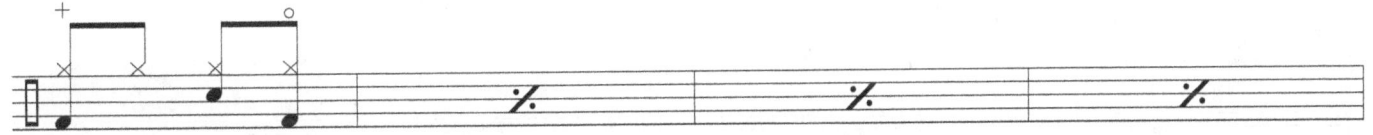

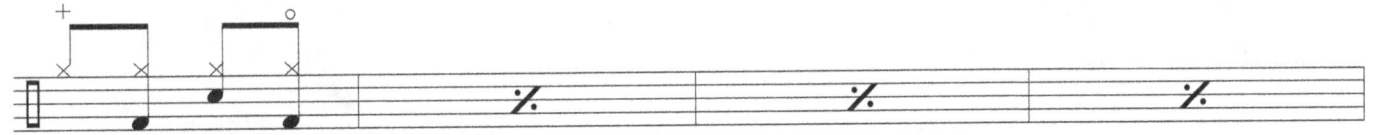

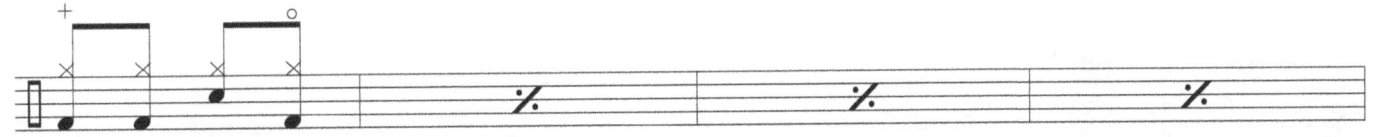

The next exercise uses 1/8th note bass drum placements with hi-hats closing on beat two (snare drum).

Example 8j

The next exercise uses 1/8th note bass drum placements with 1/16th note hi-hats closing on beat one. Again, the plus sign is relevant after the first repeat.

Example 8k

The final exercise uses 1/8th note bass drum placements with 1/16th note hi-hats closing on beat two (snare drum).

Example 81

Routine Nine – Drags and More 3/4 Grooves

This routine introduces drags, both as technical exercises and in fills, along with more 3/4 time grooves. But first, let's play our last exercise with 1/8th note accent phrases. As before, focus on the melody when moving to the toms and keep the unaccented snare notes as quiet as possible.

Example 9a

Now add the bass drum.

Example 9b

Next, you're going to work on drags. As with flams, it's important to focus on the main note (the big one), not the grace notes (the small ones). Make sure the grace notes bounce cleanly to create two clear strokes, not a buzz.

Stickings are shown for the main notes only, since that's where your focus should be. Grace notes are always played with the opposite hand. Flip the stickings when you repeat each exercise.

Example 9c

Now play double strokes while moving around the kit. This rudiment is sometimes referred to as *drag taps*.

Example 9d

Once again, play the bass drum in the gaps between the notes – a useful technique for rock and pop fills.

Example 9e

The next exercise adds movement to the half-open hi-hat and crash cymbal. Drags can be used to embellish crash and hi-hat accents.

Example 9f

The following two exercises use a technique which, for want of any better description I've come across, I call *single stroke drags*. These are not traditional snare drum rudiments, but are something specific to playing drum kit. They are very effective and can be used in all types of music. You may recognise the sound of this example from *We Will Rock You* by Queen.

Example 9g

Example 9h

Now apply these drags to standard fills. If you have two or more crash cymbals, alternate between them as you go through the exercise.

Example 9i

To finish this routine you are going to revisit some 3/4 grooves, but this time with triplets on the hi-hat. These beats could also be written in 9/8 time. Use the triplet phrases from routine five for your fills.

Example 9j

Finally, apply the shuffle pattern to the hi-hats, as covered in routine six. Use the same shuffle fill phrases you practised there.

Example 9k

Routine Ten – Buzz Rolls

This final routine is all about buzz rolls – a great skill to develop. Keep the sticks low, close to the drum, and don't drag the sticks across the head. Stay relaxed but squeeze the grip slightly and apply a little downward pressure, as if you're pressing the sticks into the drum. Make each buzz note as long as possible. A smooth, continuous roll comes from overlapping the buzz notes. The longer each buzz is, the less speed you need.

Listen carefully to the audio to hear how this should sound. Start by focusing on the sound of each buzz. Aim for a consistent tone from both hands.

Example 10a

Now work on seventeen-stroke, nine-stroke and five-stroke rolls, on both hands. Make sure you don't accent the final single stroke. It should feel like part of the roll and provide a clean cut-off.

Example 10b

Now add the bass drum. Focus on the pulse and try to settle into a groove. Imagine you're playing in a marching band.

Example 10c

This next exercise works on switching the buzz on and off. Make sure the dynamics stay even between the buzz notes and single strokes.

Example 10d

Now add the bass drum. Again, feel the groove and imagine you're marching.

Example 10e

Now take the concept further by switching the buzz on and off every two notes while playing continuous 1/16th notes.

Example 10f

Next, switch the buzz on and off one note at a time. This takes a high level of stick control.

Example 10g

Now apply buzz notes to triplets. As in routine five, triplets cause the hands to alternate each beat. Beats one and three fall on the right hand, beats two and four on the left. Keep this in mind as you play.

Example 10h

Now work on this variation, switching every two beats, then one beat.

Example 10i

Now work on seven-stroke and thirteen-stroke rolls. As before, don't accent the single stroke at the end, it should sound like part of the roll.

Example 10j

These next exercises include mixed meters. It's easy to rush the triplets, so focus on the pulse and imagine you're marching or dancing.

This exercise uses seventeen-stroke and thirteen-stroke rolls.

Example 10k

This exercise uses nine-stroke and seven-stroke rolls.

Example 10l

To finish, you'll apply buzz rolls to grooves. This is where tempo becomes a key consideration. Buzz rolls should produce a smooth, even sound, but the technique works best within a specific tempo range. To stay in that range, use different subdivisions at different tempos. In short, the faster the tempo, the fewer notes you play.

Nine-stroke buzz rolls work well at slow to medium tempos, where you'd typically play 1/8th or 1/16th notes.

Example 10m

Seven-stroke buzz rolls work well at medium tempos, with triplets or shuffle feels.

Example 10n

Five-stroke buzz rolls (notated as 1/8th notes) work best at fast tempos, where you're likely to be playing 1/8th or 1/4 notes.

Example 10o

And that's it! Congratulations on completing the final routine!

Conclusion

I hope you enjoyed the practice routines in this book and have noticed an improvement in your skills. It's important to stay disciplined and practice regularly, but don't forget that playing with other musicians should always be the goal.

Learning music is a lifelong pursuit. It takes dedication, but it's deeply rewarding. The more you practice, the more you'll improve. The more you study, the more you'll understand and appreciate this great art form, and the more pleasure you'll get from your journey.

You can reach me through my website **www.busterbirch.co.uk** where you can join my mailing list to receive free practice resources and updates on future publications.

Best wishes and thank you,

Buster

If you are ready to learn more, check out Buster's other drum books for Fundamental Changes:

The Art of Comping for Jazz Drums

Odd Time Drum Groove Mastery